I'm not in my homeland anymore

Voices of students in a new land

EDITED BY SEYMOUR LEVITAN

Pippin Publishing

Copyright ©1998 by Pippin Publishing Corporation
Suite 232
85 Ellesmere Road
Scarborough
Ontario M1R 4B9

Edited by Seymour Levitan
Designed by John Zehethofer
Typeset by JayTee Graphics Ltd.
Printed and bound in Canada by Friesens

Canadian Cataloguing in Publication Data

Main entry under title:

I'm not in my homeland anymore

ISBN 0-88751-075-2

1. English language — Textbooks for second language learners.*   2. Readers — Immigrants — Canada.   3. Immigrants' writings, Canadian (English).*   4. Second language learners' writings, Canadian (English).*   5. Immigrants — Canada.
I. Levitan, Seymour.

PE1128.I438 1997   428.6'4   C97-931705-3
10 9 8 7 6 5 4 3 2 1

DEDICATION

This book is dedicated
to
the ESL students of Vancouver
and to their teachers.

Acknowledgements

We are especially grateful to Catherine Eddy, Supervisor of the Oakridge Reception and Orientation Centre of the Vancouver School Board, who initiated the "Memories" Writing Project and assembled and inspired the Project Team; to Hugh Hooper, District Principal of English as a Second Language from 1990-97, our sponsor and enabler, whose support and generosity kept the book alive; and to Neil Horne, Associate Superintendent for Marineview Area of the Vancouver School Board, who made it possible for the book to be published.

We are also grateful to Manjula Topiwala of the ESL District Office for her patience and measureless assistance with the typing and correcting of the manuscript; and to Sandra Montgomery of the ESL District Office and Elizabeth Trujillo of the Oakridge Reception Centre for additional assistance with the preparation of the book.

We also wish to thank secondary ELS teacher Carol Nakonechny for joining us during the second year of the Project and providing a number of pieces that were included in the book; art teachers Yasna Guy and Richard Laurence for student drawings; and we are indebted to photographer Joshua Berson of Vancouver for his photos of the students who participated in the first year of the Project.

In addition we wish to thank Jonathan Lovat Dickson of Pippin Publishing for his judicious, light editing of the text and his respect for the voices of the student writers.

Paul Kim's poem "Changes" and a number of other passages from the book were used by the Vancouver Youth Theatre in their production of "New Canadian Voices." "Changes" was set to music and may be familiar to many readers of this book as a song.

"A Very Sad Day In My Life" appeared in "VAST Quarterly," Fall & Winter 1991. "I Arrived Too Late" by My Tang was retold in a different form by her younger sister Christine and printed in "Education Leader," November 6, 1992.

Introduction

I'm Not in My Homeland Anymore originated with the belief that our English as a Second Language students have experiences that need to be told, memories that need to be shared. This belief led to the "Memories" Writing Project.

Catherine Eddy, at that time ESL Coordinator for the Vancouver School Board, assembled a project team of seven members. I was the project facilitator and, eventually, editor of the book, and there were six secondary ESL teachers — Steve Dunbar, Sybil Faigin, Geri Lathigee, Anne Sander, Linda Saunders and Edna Schuerhaus — who guided their students through the writing process from the thinking and discussion phase through drafting and revision. We met regularly to discuss teaching strategies, to share examples of our students' work and to clarify the project's aim, which was to have a book preserving the authentic voices of our student writers. *I'm Not in My Homeland Anymore* is the result.

We believed that a student's writing should be corrected and revised only up to, but not beyond, the level of her or his real ability. My role as editor was mainly to provide structure to the book as a whole, to each of its sections and to individual pieces by cutting passages only in order to clarify meaning or to heighten the impact of the writing. Within that structure we wanted to preserve the student's own voices, allowing each ability level to speak in its own way. And so, with beginning and early intermediate writing, we avoided revisions that would make the diction too sophisticated, the idiomatic usage too smooth, the syntax too fluent. While our advanced writers produced some truly remarkable and intensely moving work, even they occasionally misused words and bungled idioms or complex structures, since they weren't yet entirely fluent in their new language. We felt that this should show. *Each* writing level represents accomplishment, revision and learning up to a certain point, and by letting that show we will, we hope, legitimize the work of all the students at various levels who will be using this book.

About the students' voices. Often eloquent, sometimes they are intensely so. There are numerous passages left uncorrected because they are powerful enough as they are: the sound of the midnight market "is shaking in my head," "Can you imagine what happened? It was out of my expectation," "they say strong things and it will punch my nerves," "a smooth feeling came into my heart."

These are nearly all emotional passages, but there are even stronger ones. For example, in "A Very Sad Day in My Life" the writer says "I saw his head throw many blood." He lacks the words to express the horror of the situation, yet the very simplicity and helplessness of his language gives it its power. Other passages are lyrical. For instance, Scarecrow's "It's at variance with reality. It's grim reality" is typical of his whole piece which has its own lyrical integrity and was left uncorrected.

About the structure and tone of the book. There are three main sections: "Home," "Leaving," and "New Country and Strange Nation," framed by an introductory and a concluding poem offering reflection at a distance on the themes of uncertainty and hope implicit in the later sections of the book. Though they express opposing emotions, both look forward to the time after immigration. The book's main sections are arranged to stimulate discussion, to give the reader some sense of the complexity of opinions and feelings that arose as students wrote about their experiences. For example, the pieces on schools begin with descriptions of the routines of the school day; then, bit by bit, there are varying responses to the problems of crowded classes, harried teachers and end-of-year examinations, building to an evaluation of the whole system of education experienced by the students, with strong opinions pro and con intentionally juxtaposed in such pieces as "Yen Ping." As with other segments dealing with topics like families, camps and North America, this will give students using the book a basis for discussion, writing and the evaluation of their own school experiences.

There's a range of subject matter, from the cooler to the more intense. Some topics evoke an emotional, others a factual response. We never prompted the students to reveal private experiences that they or their families might hesitate to share, but we still wanted their writing to be personal. They were never asked to report on a given subject, but to tell what they knew from their own experience, to write about things they themselves had witnessed, lived and felt, so that their writing would not be impersonal but honestly subjective.

While there's much information there's also much emotion in this book, evident as students tell about strong attachments, deep feelings of connection, friendship, family bonds, immersion in ceremony and festival. And the emotion of the writers themselves and that which they evoke in their readers is entirely compelling as they tell about the nightmare of war and the closeness of death, of the desperation of being adrift at sea with no one willing to help, of stagnating in a camp waiting for resettlement, of the fear of government surveillance, of the relief as they start for their new homeland. And there are the mixed emotions, the bittersweet reactions to the new land, the gain and loss, the enormous freedom and wonder, the loss of language and identity, the self-blame, humiliation, loneliness, and feeling of emptiness. Paul Kim's opening and closing poems express these mixed feelings, but with the healing touch of the lyric form.

The students who participated in "Memories" wrote at the beginning of this decade, referring to the wars, revolutions and expulsions of that time. While some of these may have ended, (or not, as in Cambodia's case), the terror, the pain, the loss, the anguish, the shock — the entire mix of refugee experience — is, unfortunately, not and never can be outdated, remaining an unhappy fact of current politics around the world. Among our immigrant students today are many who have had these same bitter experiences and who will connect with those of the writers.

Intended for both ESL and non-ESL students, *I'm Not in My Homeland Anymore* can serve as a basis for discussion and as a model for other "memories" writings. We hope that ESL students will feel that their own experiences merit recognition and validation through this book, and that the teachers and counsellors who work with them will find that it helps the process of communication between the newcomers and the strange nation to which they have now come. We also hope that the book will offer ESL teachers a model of writing that is instructive to *their* students — writing both informative and personal, revised with respect for the voices of the students in emotional and lyrical passages.

Finally, we hope that non-immigrant students will find the book instructive, encouraging in them a thoughtful comparison of cultures, of educational, social and political systems and of matters close to home, like friendship and family bonds, helping them understand something of the losses and nightmares of other lives lived outside the safety of North America not as stories in the news, but as the personal experiences of their fellow students.

Seymour Levitan
Vancouver, British Columbia
August, 1997

Contents

CHANGES

Paul Kim / Korea

I'm going through changes
I'm here
On the bridge
Between child and adult
Between East and West
Between light and darkness

Broken watch
Broken landmark
A free bird in the desert

Do you know what you are?
I don't know what I am
I'm just going through changes

And - - -

Please, let me be a bridge

HOME

School and Friends
Family
Where I Lived
Ceremonies and Beliefs

School and Friends

SCHOOL AT THE TOP OF A HILL

Linda Han / Korea

My first school was at the top of a hill. Winter time was the best season. The reason was that there was a lot of snow, and when the snow melted and the temperature dropped, it turned to ice, so while walking up the hill there was a chance of falling and sliding down. After school, going down the hill was just as much fun as going up the hill. Sliding, slipping or falling down. Either way, it was fun.

In Korea every elementary school pupil had name tags. The design of the tags was different for every school. They had the school's name, your name, your grade and home room number. When you reached the gate, the patrol — some Grade 6 students — checked if you had one on or not.

As you entered the gate two things stood out. The first thing was the huge field with no grass. Instead it was full of dirt and small rocks, which made a lot of dust on hot dry days or windy days. Second, the two school buildings, holding an enormous number of students.

There was no gym for P.E. or assembly, so we used the field. Assembly was held once a week and all the students in each class had to line up according to height. We sang the Korean national anthem, listened to the principal's speeches, and then did some exercises. The field was also used for sports days.

When we entered the school we had to change to white, clean shoes, which we carried with us every day. We had to bow every time teachers passed by. There was only one chalk board in front of the classroom. The desks were made for two. We weren't allowed to sit where we wanted. We had to sit by height with a boy and a girl at every desk, boys sitting on the right side.

School was open Monday to Saturday. Saturday was the most exciting day because we had shorter hours and had art as well as music. After school everybody lined up side by side and we waxed the floor until it was shiny and clean, talking and laughing while doing the work.

SCHOOL GUARDS

Benson Lo, Wilson Wong & Cheryl Chok / Hong Kong

If you were to fall asleep and wake up in front of a high school in Hong Kong, the first thing you would notice is a high metal fence or a wall of stone or brick. This is to prevent strangers from entering. In front of the school there is a guard, whose job is to look after the school, to make sure that there are no strangers standing in front of the gate, and to let the students enter.

The school must be kept under guard at all times. This is no problem because some of the janitors live at the school. They have no home or family, so their co-workers become their closest friends. Most students in Hong Kong who have spoken with them say they are very kind.

THERE ARE A LOT OF STUDENTS WHO NEED TO TALK

Christine Lee / Korea

In Korea, there are 50 to 60 students in each class, so sometimes the teacher can't control them or remember all the names. When students don't finish their homework or are too noisy, teachers get very angry and send them out of the classroom or hit them with a small stick.

Korean teachers aren't very concerned about the students, for there are a lot of them. They are too busy just thinking of teaching. Some Korean teachers say "stupid students" to the ones who get low marks. Teachers always go home late because they have to attend meetings every day after school.

From time to time, Korean students decorate their teacher's desk with flowers. If a teacher is very famous, students also fill that teacher's vase with beautiful flowers or give them a present because they want the teacher to remember them.

Korean students have to work very hard for their tests. They don't have enough time to talk with their teachers about their worries or problems, and they don't have time to enjoy anything else, so they feel a sort of stress. Teachers try to talk with them, but the big problem is that there are a lot of students who need to talk.

MY BEST FRIEND'S SCHOOL LIFE

Sarah Kang / Korea

I want to describe my best friend's school life in Korea. Her name is Won-Hee. She is 18 years old and in her final year in my old high school. She wants to be a reporter. She gets up at six in the morning. Schools starts at 7 a.m. We have seven classes a day and extra study time until 10 p.m. After school she goes to the library to study. She finishes her homework and prepares for the university entrance exam. She goes home at 1 a.m. and eats and then goes to bed.

It is her daily life.

MY JUNIOR HIGH SCHOOL IN TAIPEI: YEN PING

Charlie Chang / Taiwan

My junior high school in Taipei is near the flower market. If you want to buy some beautiful flowers, just walk across the road, then you can choose whatever flowers you want. Above the market, there's a highway.

As you might know, Taiwan is a small island; its population is 20 million. Everywhere is full of people, especially in

Taipei, the capital. There are more than two million people living in Taipei. Because Taiwan is so small, people have to know how to use space well. For example, under the highway there's the flower market with some parking spaces. Of course, a school near a highway isn't a good thing. Sometimes, when the teacher is telling you something important, if there's a truck driving along the road, you won't know what the teacher just said, and you might even miss your homework.

All students in Taiwan must take an entrance examination to see if they can study in a senior high school. Which school you go to depends on the grades you get in the tests. Good grades mean you go to a good school. Bad grades mean you go to a bad school. If you get very bad grades, you will have no school to study in. If the worst school standard is 500/700 and you get 472/700, then you will have no school to study in. If you are a good student but you are not careful in the tests, you won't study in the best school.

Lessons in Vancouver are much easier than the lessons in Taiwan. All the things I learn here are just like a review. The math I learn here is just like the lessons I studied in Grade 8 in Taiwan, but here I'm doing Math 11 (Algebra)! The science I study here is also just like the lessons I studied in Grade 8. Maybe the things we learned in Grade 9 will not be taught until university in Canada. So that's 70% of the reason the students from Taiwan can get 95% or even higher grades here and don't have to study as hard to get good grades as they did in Taiwan. I just spend lots of time trying to remember hard English words, like experiment, cells, microscope, and so on.

In Taiwan you can hear the voice of the teacher or the voice of the stick which is used to hit students. But since I came here, I haven't heard any voice of sticks. People tell me that if teachers hit kids, they might lose their jobs.

In Taiwan teachers give you lots of homework and many examinations. You won't have time to relax. But here teachers give you very little homework. Every day here is like summer vacation. We play from 3:30 to 7:30, study from 7:30 to 9:30, and we still have lots of time. Besides, the wonderful teacher can't hit kids, so not everyone wants to study hard. It seems as if teachers really don't care about what grades students get.

("Yen Ping" was given to a Senior English class to read and comment on. Their responses were given to the author who, in turn, added points of clarification.)

I'm back again! Lots of you asked why I am here, why I didn't stay in Taiwan and study if the Taiwan school system is so much better. Well, part of the answer is that Taiwan has a conscription system. Every male must become a soldier for 22 months after graduating from high school. The problem is that it is very bitter in the army. In Taiwan, a soldier in the army must practice shooting many kinds of guns, learn field operations, train for secret missions, practice landing by parachute, and so on. Sometimes you might get hurt. Taiwanese try to send their kids to other countries to "escape calamity."

I can explain why I say teachers here don't seem to care what grades students get. In Taiwan we had lots of tests — little quizzes, weekly tests, monthly tests, final tests. For example, in my school, we had more than 160 examinations a year. We always calculate the average of all the students in one class and make a comparison with other classes. If 3A got a 78% average in Math and 3B got 75% average in Math, we'd always say that meant the teacher who teaches 3A Math is better. Taiwanese teachers want their students to get good grades, and always give their students pressure or lots of tests. Since I came here, I have never seen a teacher hit a student or give students pressure, so sometimes I have to ask myself: "Is a teacher here not good? Or are teachers here so kind simply because they don't mind what grades you get?"

THEY CAN ONLY BE ANGRY IN THEIR HEARTS

Emily Chien / Taiwan

In the primary school in Taiwan, teachers often hit the little children with big, thick sticks if they do something wrong. In high school the situation is the same. Teachers strike students if they are dissatisfied with the students' work or behavior. Students are left feeling terrible and insulted, but they can't do anything to their teachers. They can only be angry in their hearts.

Tests present another problem. In Taiwan, if students want to enter high school, they must pass the national tests. These tests are based on all the courses taken during school. It is very difficult to prepare for all the tests, so students become diligent and hard-working. They are very nervous about the tests and worry that if they can't get good grades and go to a good school, their relatives will be angry or laugh at them. These tests make sure that students get no pleasure from either schools or studying.

THERE'S SOMETHING WRONG WITH THE SYSTEM

Charlie Cho / Korea

There's something wrong with the education system in Korea and I'd like to describe it.

In Korea school starts at 7:30 a.m.. There are 60 students in every classroom. Students stay in the rooms and the teacher changes classes. The subjects always include Korean, Mathematics, English, French, Physics, Chemistry, Physical Education, Social Studies, History, Music, Art,

Geography, Technical Education and Biology. The subjects are never chosen by the students.

There are always too many tests. The final test lasts for five days. It's hell. We have to study all the time in order to go to university. We study six days a week and have nine 50-minute blocks each day. Studying in Korea means memorizing. It is very different from the system here.

The spirit of unity in the classroom and the ability to make lasting friendships are the two good things about school in Korea. Sometimes the teacher hits the students, but the students don't hate the teachers; they show only respect.

FAMOUS SCHOOLS

Sylvia Chok, Jasmine Chok, Connie Keung, Monica Tang / Hong Kong

Children start school in Hong Kong at three or four years of age. If their parents are famous or rich, they can insist that the children be placed in a famous kindergarten. (The schools also provide a simple test to the kids. If they get good results, they may be accepted, even if their parents are poor.)

If students graduate from a famous kindergarten, most of them will study at a famous primary (elementary) school. After six years, students have to undergo a Government Public Examination. They are given a student number and their parents make a choice of secondary schools from the school lists. The students with the highest grades are grouped together, and the computer uses the Lucky Draw method to decide which school the student will go to. Most parents want their children to get into a famous school because the standards at these schools are so much higher; they want to be proud of them when they tell friends which school their children are attending.

HIGH SCHOOL IN TAIWAN

Tom Yeh / Taiwan

In Taiwan, most students ride their bicycles to school because there aren't any local buses around. Schools start at 7 a.m.

Everyday at 8 o'clock, pupils have to clean the school. They clean washrooms, tables, floors, stairways, windows and doors, and take the garbage out. After that, they go to the field and do exercises. Then they go to class.

Teachers are extremely mean. They think that students are lazy and never try their best, so they give students lots of work in class and test reviews for homework. All the courses are very difficult. Only a few students get over 90% on tests. If anyone gets under 60%, they go to "Basic Classes", which give more work and are very difficult.

Some students who fail the tests become crazy or kill themselves. You often read about it in the newspapers.

After a test, students have to have an envelope and stamp ready for the teacher, who mails the test home so that parents know how well their child did in school. Do you know what will happen if you fail the tests? You will get hit and a big slap on your face, and you will have to study harder, even during eating time. Sometimes parents scold their children seriously.

There are over 50 students in a class in Taiwan and sometimes teachers have a hard time running the class. But students co-operate, they don't ask too many questions, they just help each other after school in the library. Sometimes teachers tell jokes for a few minutes or do something interesting like games, drawing or singing, so that the students won't have a hard feeling whenever the teacher comes into the room.

"GOOD SHOT"

Mino Kaye / Korea

I was in a private school in Korea and there weren't many students. Here it's easy to make friends and easy to break friendships, but in Korea it is hard to make friends and hard to break friendships. When we make friends, we take a long time and we give our affection deeply. I really miss my friends, and I really miss my high school art teacher, too. He was very kind and always worried about his class.

His nickname was 'Good Shot'. This doesn't mean that he liked to hunt or was an Olympic shooter. It means that he always threw his chalk at us when we chattered loudly with our friends during the class. When he heard noisy sounds coming from his students, he first pretended that nothing had happened. Then he would break a couple of long chalk pieces for shooting. Finally he would turn back and throw the chalk quickly at us. It was always a perfect shot. My friends and I really hated those chalk bullets. But it was very funny; it was a kind of little war between the students and the teacher.

KOREAN STUDENTS

Christine Lee / Korea

In Korea, my friends and I always joined hands or put our arms around each other when we walked around. All Korean students do that, especially girls. But I don't do that here because I don't have such good friends yet, and I have never seen that done in Canada.

ORDINARY DAYS

Yukiko Takehira / Japan

I remember sports day last year. The night before it was raining and all the decorations were ruined. Our class teacher told us to come at 6 o'clock the next morning. The next morning my mother called me. It was too late to eat because I'd promised to meet my friends at 5:45. My mother gave me a piece of tasteless bread, and I dashed downstairs to meet my friends. Nobody was there. I ate my piece of bread, and then they arrived. It turned out that they'd taken time for breakfast!

When we got to school, it was still dark and my hands were almost frozen. About an hour later our work was finished and the students started arriving.

First there was a march around the field. I was tall, so I had to walk at the head of the line. I was strained and nervous. When we finished the march, we returned to our seats and the events started. I joined in a few games and one dance. We had practiced hard for the dance before sports day so we weren't nervous. Our team didn't get any prize, but it was still a big day in my life.

I didn't really like my classes at school, but I liked my friends. Every day was ordinary, but there were both happy and painful things which happened. What I miss most about Japan are the ordinary school days.

HOW TO FIND A BOYFRIEND IN KOREA

Judie Ahn / Korea

I'll tell you how to find a boyfriend in Korea. There are many different all-girls and all-boys schools in Korea, so it's not easy. One popular way is a "meeting". The same number of girls and boys meet and decide on a partner. The meeting isn't a party and there is no dancing. The students just talk and get to know each other.

Here's one way they decide on a partner — boys put their personal effects on the table and each girl chooses one. They don't know whose it is. Then the boys tell them, and so they find out who their partner will be.

Some couples stay at the place where they meet and some go to parks or restaurants. If they are interested in each other, they exchange phone numbers and become good friends.

"I ONLY LIKE YOU"

Rin Cha / Korea

What I miss most about Korea is my girlfriend. I really like her and she likes me; we love each other. We met one year and six months ago. She is 18 and I'm 17, but it is the same because my birthday is an early birthday. I didn't like girls before I met her; I only liked music. She is cute, kind, and very tall. I always bantered with her, but she understood me because she knew that I was her true love. We were always together because we were promised to each other. I wasn't afraid of anything in the world when we were together.

I remember the first time I met her in a restaurant. She gave me chocolates and a red rose. She said to me, "I like you." I didn't know that she liked me because she had many stupid boyfriends. Then she said to me, "I *only* like you." My mind was flying clear around the earth. I was very happy and crazy at the same time, but I couldn't express that to her because it is the rule. Girls are very strange animals, so I don't express my thought to any of them; instead I keep cool.

I said to her, "I don't like you because I love you."

She laughed and answered, "I didn't like you before, but now I like only you. You are different from other guys. When I saw you the first time, I thought you were a bad boy and a little bit crazy because you do not study much, you like Heavy Metal music, and you like many bad things. Now, however, I know more about you."

A fire was burning inside each of us. I knew some girls before, but I didn't have a real friend. We will be true to each other.

I always said to her, "You are mine."

I HAD RUN AWAY

Paul Kim / Korea

What I miss most about Korea is my best friend. We went to the same schools for ten years, but we weren't close friends until high school.

After junior high, I had an intolerable time. I thought no one understood me and everyone in the world was a hypocrite and my enemy. I needed someone who could understand me. We became good friends at our discussion group about literature. We had similar ideas. We talked about many things: the world, God, people, love and private secrets. He taught me how to love people, how to make my own way, because I hated all people.

Once, he and I stayed together all night long at the park. It was during the summer holidays, and I'd run away from home for a week, because I had got into very big trouble with my parents, especially my father. I hated him for many reasons. I wanted somebody to talk with and needed some money for drinking, because I'd decided to be a bad guy! So I called my best friend, and he ran to me. It was getting dark, and I bought some Korean wine with his money. He didn't dissuade me. He and I started to drink and talk at the park. I told him my complaints and what I thought about my father. Then he told me his story. He'd lost his father when he was 14 years old, and he was the oldest brother in his family. This meant that he was a patriarch. And his family was very poor. Although he studied so hard, he couldn't go to university, because of a lack of money. But he was not a pessimist like me. He was trying to love all his life, even his miserable time. I could feel my humiliation very much. He was a Big Man (even though he was very short), but I had childish thoughts (even though I was the tallest guy in my class). And he understood me. Both of us talked and talked, drank and drank all night long.

FAT CAT

Alex Ching / Hong Kong

I had a fat, colourful, and lovely cat when I was in Hong Kong. It was about seven years old when I left. It was very important in my life. It was very kind. I liked to stay with it and play with it. When I was playing with that fat cat, I could forget the crummy things and be happy again. It didn't like to move at all. Even if I rolled a soccer ball toward it, it would rather be crushed by the ball than move a bit. It was too lazy to move. It liked eating or sleeping only. It liked sunlight too. It felt hungry even if it had just finished its dinner. I liked to sleep with that timid cat. It was a soft touch toy for me. It looked like a little baby when it was sleeping.

Before we came to Canada, my father decided to send it to a friend. I objected to his decision. Anyway, he is father and I am son, so my objection didn't have any effect. When we took it to the friend's home, it looked very sad because it knew what had happened. I felt that way, too. It cried very loudly when we left it alone in a strange place. Its voice was sorrowful. I was disgusted to hear that. I was too sad to say a word. I still can't forget the scene.

SNOW MOUNTAIN

Charlie Cho / Korea

My friends and I were in the same class. We spent from 7 a.m. to 10 p.m. in school. Our homes were more like inns. Sometimes school seemed like hell, but now I think it's a beautiful memory.

I remember the time we went on a trip during our winter vacation. We were 14. We went to a very famous mountain in Korea named Snow Mountain. It's a big, high, delicately constructed mountain. We were there three days. On the first day, everybody wanted to climb Roar Rock. We walked and walked and were very tired and hungry. The snow world was beautiful and very exciting. Sometimes we ate the snow. It was cool and sweet. We arrived at Rocking Stone. The pass was very slick. We made funny snowmen and had snow fights. At last we reached Roar Rock. I thought it was magnificent. We climbed up stairs covered with snow. Only one step was clean. We were afraid. It took us 40 minutes to reach the top. The top looked like heaven.

Family

CHINESE FAMILIES ARE DIFFERENT
Madeline Cho / China

In Canada, boys and girls go away from home when they're 18 and they have to take care of themselves. But most Chinese live with their family until they get married, and after a boy gets married, his wife usually lives with his family too.

In China I lived with my great grandmother, my parents, my aunts, my sister, my brother and my little cousin. In my family, we all had our rights. My parents respected us very much. Everyone could speak out if he or she didn't like the way another member of the family behaved. And the elders liked to listen to our opinions. Sometimes my father made decisions for us. He was the head of the family.

PEOPLE WERE COLD IN MY FAMILY
Tom Yeh / Taiwan

There were nine people in my family in Taiwan — two grandaunts, a grandfather, a grandmother, an uncle, an aunt, my brother, sister and me. My parents were working somewhere else, far away from home.

All the people in my family had jobs, except the children. My grandaunts owned a restaurant and they worked in the kitchen. My grandmother had a food store. Grandfather sold Chinese medicine. Uncle was a news reporter and aunt was a nurse.

People in my family didn't get together very often, because everybody worked at different times and got off very late at night. When it was Chinese New Year, everybody got together and my parents came home, but after a few days everything went back to normal. Sometimes I had the feeling that people were cold in my family. They were usually separated. Sometimes I felt crazy because people cared only about their businesses and their jobs, and too bad between right and wrong. I smoked and nobody knew.

Sometimes, even if I met my aunt, uncle or grandfather on the street, they just pretended that they didn't see me, because they were with other people and they didn't want to be distracted.

I thought my family was boring.

MY FATHER WAS MY MATH TEACHER

Julianna Cho / China

My father was my math teacher when I was in Grade 8. He was the best math teacher I ever had. He made every chapter clear and used many examples to explain. He often went to class at study block in case students had troubles with their homework. I thought he wasn't fair to me. He always gave me the last chance — he asked the other students to do the questions first. If they didn't know how to do them, he would ask me. Sometimes someone would say I'd got a test paper from my father when I was the best one in the test. But I didn't care, because that was absurd. My father never brought his work home. He said he had to relax at home. He told me that he was my teacher at school, but he was just my father at home.

MY FATHER

Convencion Ventura / Philippines

The most important person in my life was my father. His name was Eulogio Ventura. He had black, curly hair, a light complexion, brown eyes and he was medium height. He was 60 years old when I remember him. I was nine at that time. My father was a funny man in his family. He liked music, especially soft songs. He liked to dance. Any kind of

dance, he knew it. And he liked to play dominoes. He taught me how to dance, and he told me some funny jokes and sometimes we sang together. I liked my father very much because he was a good leader in our family. Sometimes he was very strict, especially about studying, because he was a retired teacher. My father and I were close to each other. Every morning we jogged to the plaza to feel and smell the fresh air. My father liked me to sing his favourite song every night before I went to sleep. That song is called "Kapantay ay langit". It means "My love is heaven". I liked my father very much even though I only knew him for a few years.

THE FIRST TIME I WAS ALONE WITH MY DAD
Kim Chi Lai / Vietnam

My dad is the only one in my family who got stuck in Vietnam. My dad and I were not close since the day he got divorced because my mom wouldn't let me see him. I remember when I was about nine years old on Children's New Year's Eve. That night my mom went somewhere. I was playing with my friends and I saw my dad calling me from afar. I felt so happy. I ran to him. He asked me if I could go to the store to buy some toys because on Children's New Year's Day kids usually get new toys. I said that I would love to go. We went and bought a lot of toys and after that we went to eat ice cream and looked at stars in the sky. At last my dad brought me home and we said goodbye to each other. We felt like we were never going to see each other again.

That was the first time I was alone with my dad. It's the most important memory of my life. From that time, I visited my Dad once a month, but when I was going to leave Vietnam I didn't even have an opportunity to tell him so, because my mom was afraid that he would tell the police. I haven't seen his face for three years. We just talk to each other in a piece of paper. I wish that Vietnam had phones like other countries so I could communicate with him easier.

MY GRANDMOTHER

Itzel Roblero / Nicaragua

My grandmother's name was Maria Isabel Arceyuth, but everybody knew her as Chepita.

She was very tall, and I always saw her as elegant. For me, she was the most beautiful grandmother in the world. She'd taken care of my brother and me since we were born because my mother had to work. My mother was the only child who lived with my grandparents, that's why we were so important to my grandmother. She gave us whatever we wanted. She was so special for us that I think I loved her more than I loved my mom.

In December 1985 my grandmother had to have an operation. She was well after the operation, but then she began to get horrible stomach-aches, so my aunts, my mom and my uncles decided to put her in a special hospital. They had to pay a lot of money because it was not at the order of the government.

I gave all my savings. I know it was a small amount of money, but for her I gave everything. No one cared about the money we were spending because what we wanted was for her to get well. School was over, but all my friends were with me all the time.

One day I went to see her at the hospital. I really didn't want to go into her room. I was scared to look at her. But she was smiling and talking like she was O.K. I think she didn't want us to be worried about her. But we weren't children anymore, and we understood what was going on.

We asked everybody for the truth although we knew it was going to be hard. They told us that the doctors couldn't do anything more for her, and that she was going to die. Five days later, my grandmother was transported to San Jorge in an ambulance. When she got home, I ran to my room and cried. I didn't want to lose her. She was my hero.

One day she called all of us and said, "I know I'm dying, but everybody is born to die. That's why you don't have to cry for me. I leave you but I know that you loved me as much as I love you."

I told her that she was going to get well. She stopped me and said, "Don't think in impossibilities". All of us started to cry, but she was smiling. She also told us that God was with her and that she saw a beautiful lady calling her. Her last words were "Be happy, I'll always be with you, although I'll be dead".

I COULDN'T IMAGINE THAT MY GRANDMOTHER WAS GONE SO FAST

Teik Chow Kuan / Malaysia

My grandmother is the most important person in my life. In my memories, she is very kind, hard working, and helpful. Last year, she was very sick and died in an old house where she'd lived for a long time.

My grandmother's name was Chan Noi Kim. She was born in Malaysia in 1905. She married a doctor. My grandfather wasn't a western doctor, he didn't have a licence and didn't work in a hospital. He was a doctor from China. My grandfather and grandmother had nine children.

For the past two years of her life, my grandmother lived in a small town called Burga Raya. When I went to visit her, she always wanted me to sit beside her, and sometimes she gave me sweets because she thought that I was still a five year old child. When she called me to sit beside her, she told me a lot of stories about her experiences in World War Two and about her life. I also liked my grandmother to sing her songs. The songs were like poems. They were folk songs.

When I was five years old, she took care of me because my parents were too busy. I never went home from school because I liked to go around our small town and run in the fields. My grandmother was very worried about me. One day, when I stepped down from the school bus, she quickly called the neighbours to catch me and take me home. And in the end I was locked in the house all the time. But sometimes I would escape and run around again.

Three days after my grandmother died, my family and I went to her funeral. I just stood silently behind, watching. My relatives were puzzled by my strange behaviour because they thought that I would be very sad and cry. I couldn't imagine that my grandmother was gone so fast. Now all I could do was wish her good luck.

My mother told me that my grandmother loved me so much. She said that when I was a child I was very naughty and she wanted to scold me, but my grandmother always told her not to punish me. My grandmother is the person I love and who is most important in my life.

CHILDREN IN CAMBODIA

Sok Phek Hel / Cambodia [Kampuchea]

When children in my country see an older person or a teacher, they bow and ask where he or she is going. At home children have to work on the farm with their parents. We can't talk while eating. After we finish eating, our parents tell us to get the work that we did at school to show them if we did well, so we can go outside to play.

Most children in my country live with their parents all their lives. After they finish school they find a job so they can make money to help their parents.

Where I Lived

THE STAR FERRY

Tina Cheng / Hong Kong

I have been in Canada for four entire months. I miss Hong Kong deeply, especially my bosom friends, my school, and my old way of life. What I miss most, however, is the Star Ferry.

In Hong Kong, every morning I would take my heavy school bag and walk to the nearby pier to catch the ferry. Although it would still be early, there would already be many people waiting for their old friend to come. All these people, like me, preferred to take the ferry rather than the crowded mass transit railway. I hated riding the MTR, especially in the peak hours when we'd be like sardines crowded in a can. On the other hand, it was fun riding on the ferry. Although it was only a 15 minute journey, it was my most enjoyable time of the day. I didn't have to think about disgusting homework, tests or examinations. I could just close my eyes and feel the sea breeze pass over me as well as smell the freedom in the air. Beside me, other people on the ferry were enjoying treasured moments. Some were reading newspapers silently, having a short nap, or even making use of the time by studying.

I remember one night when I was riding on the ferry with all my best friends. It was the night before I left Hong Kong. After we had our dinner we decided to go to Seaside Park, on the Kowloon side, for a walk. All 15 of us marched to the pier to take the ferry. Because it was already 10:30 in the evening, there were only four people on the ferry besides us. We all took seats in the front so we could view Victoria Harbour. We seemed to have endless things to talk about. We had been classmates for more than five years; we studied together like brothers and sisters, loving and caring for each other. I hated to leave them. I also hated to leave my homeland; I knew that I had fallen in love with Hong Kong.

MIDNIGHT MARKET

George Hwang / Taiwan

I miss the noisy sound of the midnight market in Taiwan. The midnight market, always about nine or ten streets long, is only open at night. Most of the people in Taiwan were very glad to have such a market, because they were able to buy whatever they wanted after they'd finished their heavy work. Everything imaginable was displayed in the market, and it was more crowded than a department store. People also went to play games similar to those at a fairground.

I remember the first time I went to the midnight market. I was only seven years old. I hadn't had the chance to go when I was younger because I'd been living with my grandmother in a small village in southern Taiwan where there were no midnight markets. The night I went for the first time was cold and dark; the big smooth moon was in an endless sky. As the wind blew against my shoulder, the noise became louder and louder and the light grew brighter. When we finally arrived I saw that the merchants had placed the goods they wanted to sell on big squares of fabric on the ground. People were rushing and squeezing. You had to be very careful of the three-handed people who used their third hand to steal your money when you weren't paying attention. Although my mother ordered me to watch out for them, I never did see any of these people.

I miss the noise of the market very much because here everything is too quiet. No sounds remain on the street at all; I always feel lonely here. Even while I am writing this, the sounds of vendors selling clothes, people chatting and laughing are shaking in my head.

HONG KONG HOUSING

Vivien Kam / Hong Kong

Hong Kong is a small island and there are more than five million people there. Half of the people live in government owned apartments, called "estates."

The people who want to live in a government estate have to apply, and the Housing Committee will consider that family's economic circumstances and how many members it has. The House Committee is an important branch of the government. The public estates are usually lower in price than private apartments, so there are a lot of families living in them.

There are more than 60 estates in Hong Kong. Each estate has about 10 to 15 buildings. Most of them are 25 to 30 stories high. There are about 30 families living on each floor. An apartment for a family of four to six is about 500 square feet. There is a kitchen, washroom, sitting room and bedroom. The bedroom and the sitting room are combined. It just looks like a big square. If the family wants to separate their bedroom and sitting room, they have to find a lumber company, and let them divide the room. Then the room becomes very small. The kitchen is also like a little square. It can hold just two people. When the family has about six to eight members they can change to a bigger apartment, which is about 800 square feet. If the family has more than eight members, they will have two small apartments.

In each building, there are three very big elevators. They can carry about 30 people each. There are also three staircases. One of them is in the middle and the other two are at each side. In the hallways there are a lot of children playing hide-and-seek because it is a very exciting game with so many children. They can hide beside the staircase. At sunset the children's mothers will shout their sons' or daughters' names in the hall and tell them they have to come back home. After that, the hallway will change to a very quiet place.

We also have a playground inside our public estate. It's just a big garden with flowers and trees, and uses about a half of the whole estate area.

When I was in Hong Kong, I was living in a government building. In my home there were two bedrooms, a bathroom, a sitting room and a kitchen. It doesn't sound very small, but it was. My home had just 550 square feet, but that isn't bad in Hong Kong. Do you know how many square feet my room was? My tiny room was just 60 square feet! But inside that there was a bed, a chest of drawers and a desk. Therefore, no more than three people could stay in my room. But that was good enough for my family because my family just has three members.

FOOD HAWKERS IN HONG KONG

Wilson Wong / Hong Kong

You can see many carts near the schools or bus stations in Hong Kong, and different hawkers selling different kinds of food. For example, so-called "bad smell" tofu. The smell *is* bad, but it tastes delicious. Fish balls, made of shark meat, rolled with a spoon and then boiled; they taste like curry. Jellied pig's blood mixed with carrots, which tastes salty. Pancakes shaped like little eggs. Chow fun. It's cut by scissors and most people eat it with red pepper oil and soy sauce. The most expensive food is meat on a skewer. It tastes the best. Cow guts has a good taste, too. Many students buy chestnuts and boiled corn in winter on their way to school. And most people have congee for breakfast. Congee can be mixed with different kinds of food such as peanuts, beef, vegetables and fish.

When the guards of the Urban Council arrived, all the hawkers ran away because it was illegal to sell food without a license. As they ran, the hot oil would sometimes hit the pedestrians.

WE HAD OUR OWN FIELDS

Balbir Thiara / India

Canada is very different from India for my family. In my village, Mehmowal, we had our own beautiful house. In Canada, we live in my uncle's house. In my country, we had our own fields and a lot of people worked for us. In Canada, everybody in my family has to work. My father works in a wood factory and he also works on a farm. My mom works on the farm sometimes. My sister works in a glass factory and she also cleans and does other work in a medical building. I work at MacDonald's.

In India, we grew rice, corn, sugar cane, potatoes, tomatoes and other kinds of food. A lot of people worked for us in our fields. Some of them came from other, poorer states in India. Some of them lived in our village. They had to live with us because they worked for us during the day and at night also. They looked after our fields. They had to water them at night. We had machines to pump the water. The workers had to turn the valves on and off and move the pipes around. They also had to watch the machines because the electricity sometimes goes off — sometimes every day!

Besides the four or five regular workers, we needed people to pick food at harvest time. We had one boy named Jarame who worked for us for a long time. He supervised the workers. Sometimes my brother also supervised them to see how they were working.

We gave our workers a place to live, something to eat, and clothes. We paid them 400 rupees a month ($40), but we didn't give it to them every month. They wanted us to keep their money because they couldn't put it in the bank. This was because they came from other states. Every four or five years we gave them the money because they wanted to visit their villages in their states. They also sent money back to their villages for their families. We also gave them money to go to the movies.

In India, my father was a teacher in a college. He taught math and science. When I was in Grade 7 he quit and became president of the bank in our town. He never worked in the fields in our country. He went to town when we sold our food, that's all.

HUNTING SNAKES

John Nguyen / Vietnam

I lived in Hai Phong in North Viet Nam.

I would go to my friend's house to hunt snakes in the forest. My friends and I walked to a place that has a lot of short grass and we tried to catch snakes for money. To catch them we needed gloves, boots and some medicine. We covered the gloves with the medicine because it made the snake sleep right away. We used the boots to protect our legs. We walked around the forest until we saw a snake nest. The nest was a hole in dry ground surrounded by water. We all surrounded the nest, and one of my friends made the snake angry by poking a stick into the nest. The stick had an L at the end of it. When the snake's head nearly came out of the hole, he caught the snake's neck with the L stick and pulled it up in the air. One of my friends had the gloves with the medicine on them, and he grabbed the snake's head. The snake fell asleep. We pulled the fangs out by using two pieces of metal covering our thumb and forefinger. We put the snakes in a big, round basket. We caught some long and big snakes. Ten in a day. After that, we went home and sold them to the people that make "snake wine". They pull the skin off and make watch bands to sell to rich people and tourists.

Ceremonies And Beliefs

SPRING FESTIVAL IN CHINA

Madeline Cho / China

Chinese New Year is the first day of the first month of the Chinese lunar calendar. It's called "Spring Festival." The day before New Year, Chinese have family reunions and enjoy a rich dinner together, a "reunion dinner." After dinner, we would go to the street flower market open just for Chinese New Year and buy flowers or kumquats. The Chinese like to buy peach blossom because it will bring good luck, and if you put kumquat in the house it will bring riches.

People make special foods and visit their friends on New Year. People who are married give money to children and the children buy firecrackers to burn in the evening. The older boys have a party until midnight and burn firecrackers at midnight to receive the god who controls riches. The second day of the New Year, married women go back to their mothers' families with their children.

I think the happiest people are children because they can get lots of money or gifts.

THE MOON IS BRIGHTER AND FULLER

Timmy Kim / Korea

Chusok is the Thanksgiving Day of Korea. Stores are closed and all the members of the family get together and remember their ancestors. Families make "sonypyon," a rice cake. It looks like a half moon and has sesame seeds in it.

Some people wear "Han'bok", our traditional clothing. There are two kinds. The woman's Han'bok has a shirt and a long skirt and special white socks. The man's Han'bok has trousers and a vest. The woman's shirt and long skirt are usually bright yellow, red, or green. The man's trousers are usually white or blue. Han'bok is uncomfortable, so most people wear it only on special days.

On Chusok the moon is brighter and fuller than at any other time of the year. People look at the moon and make a wish. My family would go to my grandfather's house to celebrate. We would play games, eat sonypyons, look at the moon and make a wish.

WE LIGHT CANDLES OUTSIDE

Yeswin Swami / Fiji

Diwali is an Indian festival that we celebrate in October or November each year. It's a very exciting and beautiful day.

In Fiji everybody starts to prepare lots of sweets a week before Diwali. They make about nine or ten different kinds. We clean our houses, wash all the clothes, cut the grass and clean our compound. It has to be really clean. From that day on we are not supposed to cook any meat, or drink beer or rum. We eat vegetables. If you eat meat, you can't go to the temple.

On the morning of Diwali everybody wakes up early and goes shopping. We buy cards and send them to our relatives. We decorate our houses with balloons and crepe paper and decorate our compound with lights and candles.

In the afternoon we go to the temple and read the bible, pray to God and sing Diwali songs. When we come home, we light candles outside — on the steps, on the window-sills, and on the ground. Then we eat sweets and send sweets to neighbours and relatives and welcome Diwali. We call our friends and play with fire crackers. The day is very noisy. At midnight people start to beat drums and make noise and shout "Happy Diwali."

DIA de SAN JORGE

Itzel Roblero / Nicaragua

The "Dia de San Jorge" is a traditional holiday in the city of Rivas, Nicaragua. The first thing that people do is to bring San Jorge to Lake Nicaragua because old people say that he appeared on a stone near the lake. On that day both young and old people ride horses. Also they throw each other in Lake Nicaragua. There are horse competitions. They dress up the horses like a princess and put a crown on the horses' heads. The best decorated horse is the winner.

Everyone stays around the lake all day. Many people give alms. That means they give the priest all kinds of food and money. Then the priest gives it to the poor people.

They eat all kinds of fruits, especially mangoes. Also they eat chicken with rice and sandwiches. Then everybody dances the special dance of the Dia de San Jorge. They dance around a cow, and lift up San Jorge and make him dance, too.

NOROOZ

Shahram Dehkhodaei / Iran

In Iran our new year is called Norooz.

I remember when my mom taught me what it means. It was ten o'clock and 13 days before new year. I woke up and saw my mom putting some grains of wheat in a bowl that had some water in it. I asked her what she was doing and she told me that she was preparing for the Norooz. I said, "Why do you want to plant wheat"? She said "Because it will grow after one or two weeks. Then we will have one of the symbols of the new year ready." "Mom, what are the symbols of the new year?" I asked.

She answered, "We have seven symbols: meadow grass, coins, vinegar, senjid (a kind of fruit), apple, sumac (a kind of spice) and juice of germinating wheat mixed with flour. The foods that are used mean wealth in the new year, and the meadow grass means that the land will always be fertile."

Some people put mirrors on the table and that shows the honesty of the people. Others buy red fish for the Norooz, because red fish are always moving and that shows hard work.

After my mom was finished I said, "Mom, when will the new year start?" She said, "When uncle Norooz comes." He is the one who brings spring and takes winter from us — or at least, we pretend it's that way. Uncle Norooz will be here on March the 21st. On that day we will sit around the table and read the Koran, our holy book, and then we will kiss and wish each other a happy new year. The older people will give lucky money to the younger people, then we will go to our relatives' houses. The celebration continues for 13 days.

GETTING MARRIED IN HONG KONG

Kenneth Tang / Hong Kong

First the parents show their son or daughter to the other parents' son or daughter. If the man likes the woman and the woman likes the man, they start going out with each other. When both sides agree, they prepare to get married.

First, the man and his friends or brothers have to go to the woman's house. The woman and her friends have to lock the door and ask for an envelope of money. It's usually about two thousand Hong Kong dollars. The woman and her friends share the money. Then they open the door for the man, and the man and the woman get down on their knees and give a cup of tea to the man's parents first and then to the woman's parents, and then they get married. Afterwards they go to a church as the English do.

A NEW BABY

Joyce Chan / Hong Kong

In a Chinese family, a newborn baby is very important, especially a boy, because he carries on the family name. When a woman has a new baby she has to follow many traditional customs during the first month. She cannot wash her hair or eat bananas or drink cane sugar juice or cabbage soup because the old people say that they are "cool". The old people cook some special food for the mother, usually steamed soup, like ginseng, shark fin, chicken, deer antlers, or beef. But the most tasty one is "Vinegar ginger egg". Sometimes the mother is only allowed to eat salt eggs or vegetables with salt. They never add oil to the soup and the mother cannot eat shrimp, crab, or fish because they aren't "pure".

On the 12th day after the baby's birth, his maternal grandmother will start sewing clothes for him and will buy a gold or emerald ring which can protect him and make him lucky. About a month later, his mother must go back to her parents' home with her baby. She must pray and give thanks to her forefathers and turn on a small light which represents the new member of their family. A week before a "full month", many relatives visit the baby, and the grandparents give them some red eggs, "wife" cakes, or sweet cakes and "vinegar ginger egg". The relatives give the baby some red packets of money. On the day of the "full month", one month after the baby's birth, his parents must invite all of their relatives to a big dinner so that they can show the baby off to the relatives.

CEREMONIES FOR THE DEAD

Kenneth Tang / Hong Kong

In Hong Kong, when someone dies, the family gets a monk to make the dead man go to heaven easily. The friends of the dead man come and bow to him three times and the family bows back once to the visitors. When the Chinese monk finishes his magic-words, the family and the visitors walk around the coffin slowly. The mourning takes about two months. During that time, the men and the boys of the family wear a black ribbon, and the women and girls wear a blue barrette. They are not allowed to go to other people's houses. If they do, they bring bad luck to that person. The family has two choices — either to bury the body or to burn it and put the ashes in an urn.

In the spring and fall, there are two festivals when we go to the graves and remember the dead. One is Chin Min festival, the other is Chung Yeung.

We wake up very early in the morning to buy flowers, barbecue pork, barbecue beef, roast chicken, rice, fruit, etc. Then we go to the grave. When we get there, we light candles and burn "hell money" to the dead people. We bow down and show our respect, and we pour white wine on the grave, which means that we give a drink to the dead person. Finally, we clean the photo on the grave to clear the dead person's face. Then we have a picnic. We use the food we offered to the dead person.

Often a man will come along and ask whether you want the writing on the grave repainted, and sometimes kids ask if you want lucky paper. As you can see, the ceremonies for the dead are very complex; if one step of it is done wrong, people believe you will get bad luck for the whole year.

CROW IN THE MORNING, YOUT ON THE DOOR

Judie Ahn / Korea

Here are some Korean superstitions:

— if we see a magpie or hear it chirp in the morning, we have a hunch that a welcome guest will visit. But if we see a crow or hear it call in the morning, we believe that we'll have bad luck all day long.

— before we have a test for high school entrance, we receive "yout" from another person and we eat it. "Yout" is very sticky. If you put it on the wall, it doesn't come off. Students who have a test for university put it on the entrance. They believe that they won't fail the test, but will hold on like yout.

— brown seaweed, from which we make a soup, is very slippery, and students believe that if they eat brown seaweed soup on the day of the test, they'll fail.

LUCKY 8

Alice Pau / Hong Kong

The number "eight" is very important in Chinese eyes. Eight is "Fai," which also means money and riches. So at Chinese New Year many people use that word to congratulate others and wish someone success in business.

People in Hong Kong thought that 1988 was a lucky year. So we had a lottery named "Fai-Bo." Fai-Bo means easy riches. This lottery was opened on August 8, 1988 at 8 p.m. That was a lucky day. It happened once in one hundred years. The lottery prize money was 8,888,888.88 Hong Kong dollars.

Other things happened on August 8th. 888 pairs of lovers married. There was only one place for them to sign up for the marriage certificate, so the lovers had to wait for a long time. A bank gave money for the first two babies born on that day: one was born at 0:12 a.m., the second was born at 0:20 a.m. Those were two lucky babies!

LEAVING

War and Forced Labour
Camp
Getting Out

War and Forced Labour

WE LIVED IN A BATTLEFIELD

Silvia Escalante / El Salvador

We're from El Salvador, and have lived in Canada two years. I would like to tell you about my country.

When there was war in my country, the children were very scared. Sometimes the battles would last 12 hours and sometimes up to one and a half days. When the battle was over the children were still very scared: they didn't want to go to school, and they would shake with fear.

If my sister saw a soldier dressed in green, she would begin to shake with fear. Sometimes, when the soldiers needed more people to fight in the war, they would kidnap the teenagers from poor families, and not from rich families. Even if the teenagers didn't want to go, they were forced to go, and some of them were never seen again. My family had friends with teenage children. They were killed in front of their parents because they didn't want to go to fight in the war. Soldiers were all over our house and hiding behind our house. They would shoot at anyone they saw because the area where we lived was right in a battlefield.

When there was war in my country we had to hide under a bed, because that was the only safe place. Sometimes bombs would land on houses, and after maybe one and a half days under the bed my family would feel weak, but we didn't want to eat. We felt like we were going to die. All that noise of bombs, guns, and helicopters was terrible for the kids.

We had a friend whose son was very young. There was war at that time. There were lots of bombs and guns, so there was gas in the air. And the little boy died.

EVEN MORE THAN THAT I CAN'T DESCRIBE AT ALL

Chay Lou / Cambodia [Kampuchea]

I'm from Cambodia. For many years we lived under the Pol Pot regime, poorly and miserably. We were starving and were forced to do hard labour day and night without stopping. Pol Pot didn't give us enough food to eat. They only offered us a bowl of porridge and a bit of salt for our whole family — six people. It was not enough for us. So our parents didn't eat. They left it for us, because they didn't want us to starve. Most of the children were sick and weak, because of lack of food. Some died of hunger and illness. There were no professional nurses or doctors, no hospitals and no medicines. The bodies of the sick people were swollen and they slept on a bed until they died.

Everyday Pol Pot forced people to do ploughing and plant rice. The rice fields were about two hectares square, and the people had to finish ploughing and planting in three days. If not, they would be punished: no food for one day. Therefore they were frightened and worked hard without resting.

Pol Pot also played a trick on people and lied to them: today we'll go to work in the forest and cut trees down to build houses. All of these people were tied up and killed with the wooden stick. Their families were at home waiting for them for days and days, but didn't see them come back. People believed those people were killed and would never come back again.

Pol Pot massacred more than a million people. Those people were the engineers, scientists and teachers as well as common people.

Children didn't really have to study. Instead, Pol Pot hired stupid "teachers" who couldn't read even the ABC to teach the children. The more they taught the children, the worse the children became. The idea of Pol Pot was to teach the children to kill their own parents. It's incredible. Thirteen and fourteen year old boys were in the army. They didn't learn anything. Their brains were empty and usually they lacked morals. This was the big problem in the country.

For me, I also struggled and overcame that kind of thing. Even more than that I can't describe at all.

I ARRIVED TOO LATE

My Tang / Cambodia [Kampuchea]

I still remember the day my father left me forever. In 1975 when Pol Pot gained power in Cambodia, many people were tortured and killed. Some died of starvation. My father was one of the victims who was forced to labour under the sun and in the rain, who lived in the deepest misery and suffered so much that it made him feel life just wasn't worth it anymore. Because of excessive work and without getting enough food or rest, my father was critically abused. He stayed in bed for two straight months, haunted by hunger.

One night it was raining cats and dogs. Father had a terrible fever. I accompanied him by sitting at the side of his bed. His pale face suddenly turned toward me with the words, "If only I could taste a bowl of rice, I would die happy." He looked at me eagerly. I could do nothing. I just sat still. Tears blurred my eyes. Suddenly I saw a little alarm clock on the table. I got an idea. I seized the alarm clock and pocketed it. I started to run to another village in the torrential rain. I didn't have time to think about it. The only thing I wanted was to gratify my father's desire. I was really bold, running in the dark by myself, but nothing could frighten me at the moment. In exchange for the alarm clock, I finally got one bowl of rice. I was full of extreme joy, but very exhausted. However, that bowl of rice encouraged me, because it would give dad a happy smile that I hadn't seen for so long.

It was very early in the morning when I got back. Can you imagine what had happened? Oh, God! It was out of my expectation, I couldn't believe what had occurred. I wouldn't accept the fact, I couldn't. I almost lost consciousness when I saw the rigid body of my father. "You left your dear daughter without saying goodbye", I said to him. Tears drained my eyes again.

The bowl was still in my hand. I didn't see the rice. I only saw the brutality, corruption, and tears. I hated myself that I arrived too late to save my dad.

Whenever I recall my father's face, I feel lonely and see the darkness around me. The deepest remorse in my mind almost drives me crazy. If I had one wish, it would be that my father was alive again.

A VERY SAD DAY IN MY LIFE

Anonymous / El Salvador

I'm from El Salvador.

October the 21st, 1986, was a day that I could never forget. I remember it was Friday. When I woke up, the sun was shining and I said, "What a beautiful day it's going to be." An hour later I went to school and met my friends and we were talking and laughing. A teacher came to us and said, "You are laughing again, as you always do." After a couple of minutes we went to our classroom.

It was at 8:30 in the morning and we were in science class. A tank broke into the school and many soldiers were shooting all around, killing many students because they were supposed to kill people who were in a group that did not agree with the things that they do. It was a school where many people didn't even know about these things, but in fact, the soldiers didn't care about that. They just came to kill everyone.

When this was happening, my friend and I were looking for a way to escape, but we couldn't find one, because there were soldiers everywhere. Then my friend saw a little corner where there was a hole and said, "Let's escape there. We're safe!" We started running, but when we were almost out I saw my friend's head throw many blood and he fell down. I tried to carry him, but I couldn't, because a soldier was shooting at me. I didn't have any choice but to get away. I was very scared and I jumped out and started running without knowing where to go, but when I was far away, I began to pray to the Lord and went home.

I SAW HIM IN MY DREAM

Shahram Porsaki / Iran

I would like to describe the worst experience in my life. It started at school. The principal of Safari School talked to all the students. He asked if anybody wanted to go to the battle front and learn how to use a gun. He said, "Sign this paper and get a permit from your parents."

After the end of school, I walked home. My cousin came to me and said, "Would you like to go to the battle front?" I said, "Not really." He said, "If we go we'll have lots of fun!" But I didn't agree with him because we would play with our lives and, of course, we could be killed. Then he started to beg me. After a lot of request I said, "All right. But you have to satisfy my mother." He said, "All right, I'll do it for you." The next day we went to school and brought the permit that we got from our parents to the principal, and the principal gave us an agreement to sign. We read the agreement and signed it. After a month there were 50 guys ready to go to the battle front, and all the students' parents came to school to say goodbye to their children. There were two buses ready. All the students got on the buses. They wore special uniforms and were happy because they would be learning all about the techniques of war. The drivers started.

We headed for southeast Iran. After 10 hours we reached Koramshahr in the afternoon. We slept there. The next day a group of soldiers called "pastaran" brought us to the battle front. They gave a gun to each boy, and they taught us how to use them. After two weeks of practice, they made us into five groups of ten students each. They brought us through the war zone. My cousin was with our group. We saw lots of dead and injured people. I saw lots of dead bodies that didn't have heads, legs, or hands. And I saw a head in which the bone of the head was broken and the brain was coming out. All the students felt sick, even me.

After a few days we left the battle front. We went through the war zone again. It was afternoon, about 3 p.m. A bomb landed right next to our group. It had a sound like a whistle. The leader of our group said very loudly, "Get down!"

All the students wanted to get down but it was too late. The bomb exploded. The explosion got me and it threw me about three metres up in the air. I fell down again. I had a very bad backache. After the explosion I stood up and called my cousin, but he didn't answer me. I called him again, but there was still no answer. I went to find him. I saw him dead. His hand was two metres away from him; his arm was torn off. I saw three of the students were dead. I started to cry very hard.

After that, I went home. And I saw him in my dream.

Camp

SEVEN DAYS AND EIGHT NIGHTS

Tai Mai / Vietnam

In 1982 I left Vietnam with my two older brothers and my sister-in-law because my parents wanted me to have a better future. We left at night. We went to a small boat and it took us to a bigger boat. When I got on board, the small boat headed back to the shore to pick up the last people. Suddenly we heard a lot of guns shooting. So our Captain said, "We have to leave without them".

I was faint the night the boat left. I couldn't stand the smells of gasoline and of people throwing up. I was in the boat for seven days and eight nights. Many things happened to us during that time. First we saw a plane and we tried to signal it. The captain asked us to give him things that we didn't need, so we gave him rubber sandals and plastic bottles. He piled those things on the deck and burned them. Soon there was black smoke everywhere. But the plane left anyway. A few nights later we saw a big ship, so we came closer. The ship was bigger than we expected and we were so excited and we yelled so loud that the people on the big ship thought we were pirates and it left. It went so fast that we couldn't believe it. Soon it was just a little light in the distance.

By the next morning we were almost out of water. That day, we saw an island. The captain asked a few men to swim to shore, and they found a stream, so they came back to get some big plastic bottles. We got about four big plastic bottles of water, but it wasn't very clean.

In the evening, we saw an army ship and we waved and yelled, but it didn't see us or hear us. After that we saw lots of other ships and some of them waved at us. We were very excited, so we waved back, but none of them stopped. Finally another army ship saw us waving and yelling, so it turned and went around our boat. A man was holding a speaker. Around him there were two or three men holding machine guns. The guy on the army ship talked to our captain. He turned and talked to some of the people on our boat. More than one person in our boat spoke English, but I didn't know what they were talking about. So I went to sleep.

The next thing I knew the army ship was pulling us so fast that I could hear the waves hitting the boat very hard, and I had the feeling that the boat was going to fall apart. At night it stopped and I heard the army people say that they were on duty and had to leave us. Before they left, they gave us plenty of water, food, and gas and showed the captain the way to go to an island, but he went in a different direction.

A couple of hours later we saw little lights in the distance but we didn't know whether it was a ship or an island until we came closer. It was an island, so we stopped the boat and threw the anchor into the sea and waited overnight. In the morning we saw many Malaysians standing on the shore, staring at us. Some of them swam close to our boat to look at us. Later, soldiers came to the beach with their guns. Our captain took a few people with him to the beach. They came back soon, and I heard them say, "The soldiers said that they would give us what we need, but we have to leave or they'll shoot us." They gave us water and food and we left Malaysia and went on.

After a few days we saw another island. The captain used his binoculars to see whether anyone lived on the island. Finally he saw a house surrounded by coconut trees. There was a woman sitting next to me. She used the telescope to look at the house again, and she saw a man in a canoe coming toward us. When he got to us, the captain and some people on the boat talked to him. He said he would take us to Indonesia, but we had to give him gold, gasoline, and the captain's binoculars. We had no choice, so we decided that each person in the boat had to pay a little bit of gold. Some of the people on the boat didn't have any gold or money with them, so the captain, my brother and some friends lent them some gold, and they said that they would pay it back.

I ALWAYS THOUGHT ABOUT THE RESETTLEMENT

Can Tieu / Vietnam

I came to Indonesia in 1983 by boat with 60 other people. I lived on a small deserted island with nothing but a lot of coconut trees. I was there for a month. Then we transferred to another island where I lived for three months. I liked living there very much, because I love the sea.

Every morning at eight some of the Indonesians woke everybody to do exercises. I usually went for a swim before lunch because the beach was just in front of my barrack. Sometimes I went fishing or cutting special kinds of flowers to make soup for meals. After meals, I would look out and see the sun hanging in the sky. It looked like an egg yolk. Sometimes I sat down near a big log in front of our barrack with my friends and we played music, sang songs and told stories. I usually went to bed at 9 p.m. because at that time the water was calm. Most of the people went to bed then. Sometimes I went to the Buddhist temple at night. There was also a Catholic church, but I heard somebody say that they had seen ghosts there. I thought there could have been ghosts there because many people had died since they came to the island. Sometimes I was afraid and sometimes I wasn't. When I wasn't afraid, I used to go out and climb on some boats that had been in the dock for a few years. I liked to sit on the boat instead of going to bed. I always thought about the resettlement. That's why I couldn't go to bed early.

Later on, I transferred to the main island. When people were there, they had to make an appointment to see a delegation before going to a third country. Most of the delegation wanted to accept people with a little knowledge of English and skills. So people had to go to school and learn English and skills. If the people had relatives in the third country, they didn't need to study very hard because their relatives sponsored them and they didn't stay there very long. But the people who didn't have relatives had to stay at least one year to study and get certificates. If they weren't good enough in English, the delegation refused them and told them to spend more time studying.

A REFUGEE CAMP IN THE PHILIPPINES

Loan Nguyen / Vietnam

After we left Vietnam in the boat, we lived in a camp in the Philippines. I lived there for a year. That wasn't very long. There were people who had stayed there for over five years. They got married and had children there. They didn't have to worry about life because the governments of Canada, the United States, Australia and other countries paid for them. That way wasn't a good way for the future, and I didn't like it; I wanted to live my own life. But we had to understand them, because they didn't have any relatives in other countries. That was why they lived in the camp for many years.

Everyone had to go to school to learn English or French. Everyday at ten in the morning everyone in every family or house went to get fish and meat from the big house. One person in the family cooked for the day.

Adults went to school two hours a day and they looked after the children. Some adults had no family there. They volunteered for jobs like delivering food, letters, clothes. Some people who spoke English well volunteered to translate for us when we had to meet English-speaking officials.

Every month, cousins or friends in Canada, Australia or the United States mailed money to people in the camp. My uncle in Canada sent my family some money to buy things. People who didn't have anybody to send them money had to save money from food. When they got food, they just ate half of it and sold the other half. Some families had a lot of money, so they opened restaurants or coffee shops in the camps.

A man named Linh was head of the camp. He was loved by all the people because he worked hard to help refugees. He was fun and kind. He had to speak English well. He needed to talk to all kinds of people in English. He usually looked after the people in the camp and reminded them about the day they had to clean their houses and other things.

My camp was better than other camps. We had electricity and water. But sometimes we didn't have water, so we had to rent a truck and drive to town to get it. Every week on Saturday they showed movies outside. On holidays we had parties.

I had a lot of fun when I lived there. But it was really hot there, and I hated the hot season. I just went to school every day, I helped my mom to cook, and I played. I had a lot of friends. When my old friends left the camp, I found new friends who just came from Vietnam. We went many places outside the camp. We went picnicking, camping, and swimming on weekends. Every night I went to my friends' houses to study English.

Sometimes, we went to Filipino houses to buy coconuts. We didn't buy a lot — we just bought two and stole three. The Filipinos knew that, but they didn't say anything because they thought that we only did it for fun. They just smiled at us.

AT NIGHT THEY CAME TO TAKE YOUR MONEY

Searn Dok / Cambodia [Kampuchea]

We left Thailand in 1989 because there was too much trouble in our refugee camp. There was fighting and killing there. Our family had a hard time staying there because we were working in the camp. Some people were poor; they couldn't get jobs. These people knew who was working, who had money, and when you got paid. At night, they came to take your money. First, they asked you nicely, but if you said no, they hurt you or burned your house down. The houses were only made of bamboo and grass, so they were easy to rob; there was no protection.

HE WRAPPED MY HAND VERY TIGHT

Sambath Om / Vietnam

I had one best friend. He was a very good person. When I had something that I didn't understand he always explained it to me (or other students). We studied in the same school. He was smart and brave.

In 1982 we were about 15 years old. One day we decided to go out of the camp because we felt hungry. We didn't have enough food to eat. The camp was surrounded by Thai soldiers. My friend told me that we were getting close to the fence. He said, "I don't want those soldiers to see us at all. If they see us they might shoot us." He told me to follow him. We went step by step. We used our hands to open the wire gently. My friend said, "O.K., run!" The soldiers turned around and told us to stop right there. We didn't stop, we kept running very fast. BANG! BANG! BANG! My friend was shot in the chest. I didn't realize that he was shot. I turned around and I saw him lying on the ground not very far from the fence. He was still alive. I stopped running, went close to him and bent my knee down and picked him up. "Come on! I can't leave you alone". We stayed there together for 30 minutes. One of the soldiers was very kind and called the ambulance for us. On the way to the hospital my friend talked about everything that we did.

The ambulance stopped in front of the hospital. I picked him up and I told him not to worry, that he would be safe now. He didn't answer me. When I looked at his face he was gone. At that time I went unconscious. I remember before he died, he wrapped my hand very tight, so I know that he wanted to tell me something. But it was too late.

LAST DAY IN THAILAND

Chay Lou / Cambodia [Kampuchea]

On my last day in Thailand I had a small party and invited all my friends. It was our last chance to see each other face to face. They helped me pack my suitcases and buy special things in the supermarket, like clothes and shoes. After that, we went to a football field to play soccer. We had a good time together. My family took me for a walk to enjoy the last landscape I would see in Thailand. Then my family and friends took me to the airport. It seemed crowded around me, and everybody tried to say something to me. But I just couldn't answer each one of them, because of many people and many questions put to me. Suddenly I got in the plane, and I heard the sound of saying goodbye coming to me from the distance. It was a large bird that I was on, but it still took me 24 hours to get here.

I was frustrated and sad to leave Thailand and all of my friends. I cried a lot on the way to the new country and strange nation.

Getting Out

FENCES AND WALLS

Anonymous / Nicaragua

The most important change in my life was freedom. In my country you don't have freedom. You do what the government says. If you want to see your relatives who live in another country, like Costa Rica, El Salvador or Honduras, you have to go to the border because the government doesn't allow them to enter Nicaragua. You have to go to the border.

The border is made up of a very high wire fence. Your relatives are on one side and you're on the other. If somebody tries to cross, the police shoot them. Also, 15 year old boys can't leave Nicaragua because they have to go into the army. The government orders schools to put bits of broken glass on the walls around the school grounds, so that when the police come to get the boys they cannot escape.

EXIT VISA

Anonymous / Nicaragua

I left Nicaragua and came to Canada because my family and I were having political problems. My father had worked as a teacher in the last government, and when the Sandinistas seized power they began to take away all the people that had worked for the last government. One day they took my father, and my mother never knew where he was. I don't remember my father because I was only five years old when the soldiers took him. Then my mother began to receive messages from the soldiers saying that he was dead and that her children would die, too. My mother wanted to leave the country, but it wasn't possible for us because they said that a member of a family who had worked in the Somoza regime was not allowed to leave Nicaragua.

We had passports, but the government would never give the exit visas to my brother and me because they said that we had to live forever in Nicaragua because of my father. They said that my mother could leave, but my brother and I no.

Years went by and my mother was still receiving those awful anonymous messages. One day, my mother found a friend. He was working in the Mexican embassy in Managua, where he lived, and he told my mom that he was going to help us. This was in July, 1987. A month later my brother was followed by the police, who wanted to take him into the army, but he ran and ran as fast as he could to get home. Once my brother was in our house, they couldn't take him because if they had, all the neighbours would know. This was not good for the police because they say that they never forced young people into the army, but that is not true. They do take young people when they are just walking along or on their way home from school. My brother was 12 when the police followed him.

On August 22nd my mother's friend got the exit visa for us. We couldn't believe it. At last we were going to leave Nicaragua! We were very happy, but at the same time very sad because we were leaving our relatives we loved so much.

When we got to the airport, there were all our relatives and my friends. I felt that I was going to die because everybody was crying. Also we were worried because the police could still stop us at any time. I was praying to God for us. The hours passed and nothing happened. It was the hour to say goodbye. We said goodbye with the hope that some day we would be together. When we got on the airplane, we felt safe. We spent a night in Mexico to catch the airplane to Vancouver the next day. On the airplane to Vancouver, I was thinking about all the problems we'd had but that now we were getting a new life, freedom. My mother began to smile. Something had changed in our lives.

NEW COUNTRY AND STRANGE NATION

IN CANADA EVERYTHING IS FREEDOM

Ken Dang / Vietnam

I left Vietnam for lots of reasons. First I needed freedom of speech and freedom to travel. My country doesn't have that kind of freedom. For example, if you talk against the government, you go to jail or they shoot you. But in Canada you can say or do anything that's not against the law, and it's O.K. Also in Canada you can go everywhere you want to, and you have the right to qualify for any public position or office. If you are 18 or older, you vote in an election. Compared with my country, it is just like Heaven and Hell.

Nobody likes to leave their country. Everyone has their reasons, like me. If I didn't leave my country by now I'd be in the army. Joining the army is not fun. 95% die and 5% live, if they are lucky. In Canada you don't have to join the army if you don't want to. In Canada everything is freedom. No one can force you to do anything if you don't want to.

I think one day I would like to go back to my country to visit my friends, but my dreams will never come true. Dreams are just a feeling, like magic.

I WISH THAT I WERE A MACHINE

Gi Li Yang / China

It's terrible for me to live in another country where people speak a different language.

I was born in China. Before arriving in Canada, I'd already studied Chinese at school for nine and a half years. In six months, I would have graduated from high school in China.

Living in Canada, I've found that my English is very limited. To improve my English level, I've limited myself to reading English books and English newspapers, and I don't read or write Chinese. By doing this, I have slowly begun to forget how to write my native language. Yesterday, when I wanted to answer my friend's letter, I felt really that I was losing the balance between speaking and writing in Chinese. Facing the problem that my English is still very limited and my Chinese has decreased to a level that I couldn't believe, I ask myself what I can do about my future? If I stop studying right now, I will be garbage and no use any more in the world. Because I live here, my knowledge of English is more important than my knowledge of Chinese. Since I can't do both things equally well, I choose to give up knowing how to write in Chinese.

When I'd been in Canada several months, I still didn't understand what people were talking about in English. In my mind, they spoke too fast to hear and understand. When people asked me for things, I gave them the wrong things. When people talked to me, the only way I could answer was very simple. Sometimes, to pretend knowing English, I just answered "yes" or "no". What did people think of me? They thought that I was dumb and foolish. If I knew English, I wouldn't be a deaf and stupid person in other people's eyes.

After I knew a little English, I began to worry about my future. Wanting to graduate from high school in Canada, I have to finish English 11 and 12. Right now my English level is at only Grade 4. How long will I have to study English before I study English 11 and 12? I don't believe that I have the endurance to wait several years to graduate from high school in Canada. Even though going to university is my goal for the future, maybe I'll be too old.

I wish that I were a machine that could work day and night without having any rest. Right now I look like a boat that has lost its direction in the ocean, trying to find its way back.

JUST LIKE A BABY

Dan Li / Taiwan

To me, the day that I arrived in Canada was a nightmare. I still couldn't understand why I would bring myself to a strange place like this. I didn't know anything about Canada. Suddenly so many problems arose — my English, the culture, the names of places.

I was a happy kid who never studied hard but still was on the honour roll. Somehow I fell into a totally different world. I was just like a baby who doesn't know anything. I had to start all over again to learn how to talk. The first year was hard, really hard. Before, I was a boy who did good work in school and never worried about anything in his entire life. But after, I felt I was the worst guy in the whole school.

JUST ONE WORD

Donna Deng / China

The first day I went to Junior High in Edmonton I went to class with my niece. The students said, "Good Morning", but I didn't understand. My niece told me to say "Hi", but I was so nervous I couldn't say it aloud. A teacher asked me where I came from, and I answered, "China" — just one word. I didn't understand what the teacher was talking about. When she asked me my name, I didn't know what she was asking. I didn't know how to count from one to twenty. I didn't even know how to read the alphabet. After school I saw some girls turn on music and dance with the boys. I was so surprised because it was very different from China. In China, students wouldn't do that. If you did, and the principal found out, he would kick you out of the school.

CANADIANS

Yukiko Takehira / Japan

Canadians are vivid and strong-willed. They say yes or no clearly. They say what they want and what they like. If they hate something, and someone says he or she likes it, they still won't change their minds. Sometimes it is bad being a friend to them because they say strong things, and it will punch my nerves and feelings. For example, they might say, "That hair style looks funny" when I like that hair style. But otherwise, it is nice to have a friend like that. They won't hide their minds, thoughts and feelings, so I don't have to care about their thoughts and feelings all the time and can be open-minded, too. Anyway, I like and dislike vivid and strong Canadians. Their minds, feelings and wills are as hard as a rock.

But Canada would be a better place for me to live in if I could understand English. I feel nervous when people ask me questions. I can't understand them well. I'm frightened to speak to my friends, so I can't have a nice conversation with them. What I can only do is just laugh like crazy.

Emily Chien / Taiwan

Canadians are quiet. They don't make any unnecessary noise. Canadian drivers seldom blow their horns on the street. Canadians never shout in public places. They don't talk very much either. Especially in the residential areas. These areas are so quiet that you just hear the birds and the voice of the wind through the leaves.

Canada is a lonely place, because you play on a large, empty tennis field, you walk around a park with no people, and you run on a street where nobody passes you. These situations make you look and feel lonely.

Helen Chow / Hong Kong

Canada is a peaceful country. People are kind to each other. As to my native place, there's also no war, but it's a small city with a large population. People all live in crowded places and, due to crowded living quarters, become selfish and are easily in conflict with their neighbours.

Tina Cheng / Hong Kong

Canadians are the most polite people I've ever met. Whether you know them or not, every time you see Canadians, they ask you, "Hello! How are you today?" Every time you help them, they say, "Thanks a lot!," and when you leave, they say, "'Bye, have a nice day." At first I was very impressed by their friendliness. However, as time goes by, I'm now used to it, and sometimes I'm doubtful about the true meaning of these beautiful words. These are just their social skills. They're just wearing masks of kindness and politeness.

LONELINESS

Rin Cha / Korea

Pure English makes me a fool. I do what elementary students do. My girl friend is now a university student. I'm in high school. No fun, I never grow up. I stay a child. I don't want many things, but loneliness invades my heart and hurts my system like a razor.

When I am loneliest, I drive to peopleless places alone and listen to my favourite killing music gently like a statue. No one is beside me. Just Armageddon is with me.

No one calms my lonely soul, a drifting boat. Just I can.

Yukiko Takehira / Japan

My loneliness is like a bare tree standing between big buildings. In the morning, the streets are crowded with many people going to their business. No one notices that there is a tree. Around noon, many people go out for lunch, but most people are seeking places to eat and no one seems to notice. The tree is bare, sunlight doesn't face it.

My imagination goes far away to my homeland. I'm in my classroom. At the front of the room, there's a teacher. He's teaching the class interestingly, students are listening enjoyably. No one notices that I'm there. I want to say something to my friend in front of me, so I whisper to her. It seems she can't hear me, so I call her once more. This time I try to whisper loudly. She doesn't turn around and face me with a smile, so I shout, "Hatomi!" She doesn't turn around. No one, including my teacher, notices me. I feel like a ghost.

Scarecrow

I'm loneliest when I think about my homeland. I always think about my friends and I miss them. But it's at variance with reality. It's grim reality. I don't live in my homeland anymore. I live in Canada. It's hard for me. I always feel empty. Everybody is away from me. I can't love anybody. What do I live for? I'm left alone in all of the world.

In the rainy night, I can't hear any voice, but I hear my mind's voice, and a quiet, rainy sound, and my friend's voice. It's my alone time. It's a beautiful time to me. I'm not doing anything. I'm concentrating. My mind is crying and shouting. I'm thinking about my friends and my good times. My mind is aware, visiting my homeland. Now I can hear my friend's voice. I write a letter in my mind: "Scarecrow is always alone. Nobody visits him and he can't visit anybody. Scarecrow's life is always lonely."

Tina Cheng / Hong Kong

Leaving the ESL class is like a child losing her parents.

When I knew that I was put in the ESL class, I was very disappointed. In the first week, I was totally upset and was in a very low mood, because I didn't have many friends, and all the things around me were unfamiliar. Besides, I didn't want to be distinct from others. I wanted to be a regular student. However, after the first day of integration, the master of hell told me where heaven was. As I first stepped into the regular classroom, I could easily feel the coldness and bitterness in the air. Everyone was indifferent to me. I was standing in front of the classroom like a fool waiting for the teacher to come. I was so embarrassed that I wanted to cry out and run back to the ESL class.

As time went by, I made more friends in the ESL class, and we studied together like brothers and sisters. We cared for and helped each other. But I remain an unconcerned visitor in the regular class after six months. I talk to no one. So now I am just travelling heaven and hell, back and forth.

Alex Ching / Hong Kong

I don't have a close friend here. I am really afraid about that. It is terrible when you're in trouble or in a sorrowful need without friends to help.

I liked to go out with my friends when I was in Hong Kong. But now I hate to go out alone. I feel I am becoming a pensive person. In Hong Kong, I was famous for making jokes in school. Here I almost forgot how to make fun with others.

Emily Huang

When I am loneliest, I turn on my stereo very loud. That's my surface, but in the deep of my heart, I hope there's someone I miss who could call me and say something that could make me happy, but there isn't. I so wish there is somewhere I could go, but there isn't either. In fact, I just can sit at my desk and face the white wall and listen to the music I don't hear. Sometimes my father calls me, but it's no help, it just makes me miss my father more and more.

SNOW

Simon Tran / Vietnam

Suddenly my pen broke while I was writing and I felt a great fear come over me. My super-human brain told me something unusual is going to happen today, but it didn't tell whether it would be helpful or harmful for me. After school I went to the bus stop. I looked up at the sky. A smooth feeling came into my heart, and that made me a little bit relieved because this always means something good is going to happen.

I got on the bus and sat in the back row. I was wondering why everybody on the bus had an umbrella. I really wanted to know why, but I couldn't speak any English, and I was too shy to ask other Orientals on the bus. I just kept quiet. I felt a strong wind blow, and there were little white things dropping from all over the sky. I forgot to get off even though the bus had gone two blocks past my house. After a moment, my helpful brain told me it was snow. I didn't know what to do because it was the first time in my life I saw, touched, and tasted snow. I was even happier than if I had found gold.

I'M READY

Simon Tran / Vietnam

I felt happy and excited when we arrived in Calgary. We walked out of the airport following the other people because we came here without any English, so even the word 'exit' was unknown to us. Everything made me feel confused. I thought, "Pretty soon I'll see my brother, and I haven't seen him for years. I wonder if he has changed a lot? Is he fat? thin? tall? short? strong? weak? handsome?" Nervously I held my mother's hand and hoped she could make me feel better.

There was a gentleman calling us. He was about six feet tall and a little fat. My brother is a generous person. My parents were crying. They were so sensitive. I almost did, too, but I acted like a mature young man (I was 13) and faced my brother with a smile and said, "Hi." We kept talking until the sensitive moment was gone.

When I walked out of the airport, I felt extremely cold. The snow made the land all white, just like a white-coloured world. During the car trip, I saw very few people on the street. There were many beautiful stores and funny houses beside the streets. In this white world, I knew there was an exciting new life waiting for me, and my self-confidence told me I'm ready to get it.

THE NEW DAYS

Paul Kim / Korea

If the new days come,
my free soul
will play in the fresh field
like a little deer,
my tender mind
will have endless peace
across the blue lake.

If the new days come,
no more tears,
now the sounds of the bell
in my land of sadness,
my dropped tears
will change to sweet fruit
in your garden.

If the new days come,
the bird which was lost
will come back over the hill
with sunshine,
the white dove
will make a nest in my calm mind
with the green leaf.

The days are coming.

Titles & Authors

TITLE	AUTHOR	COUNTRY
CHANGES	Paul Kim	Korea

HOME

SCHOOL AND FRIENDS

School at the Top of a Hill	Linda Han	Korea
School Guards	Benson Lo, Wilson Wong & Cheryl Chok	Hong Kong
There Are a Lot of Students Who Need to Talk	Christine Lee	Korea
My Best Friend's School Life	Sarah Kang	Korea
My Junior High School in Taipei: Yen Ping	Charlie Chang	Taiwan
They Can Only Be Angry in Their Hearts	Emily Chien	Taiwan
There's Something Wrong With the System	Charlie Cho	Korea
Famous Schools	Sylvia Chok, Jasmine Chok, Connie Keung, Monica Tang	Hong Kong
High School in Taiwan	Tom Yeh	Taiwan
"Good Shot"	Mino Kaye	Korea
Korean Students	Christine Lee	Korea
Ordinary Days	Yukiko Takehira	Japan
How to Find a Boyfriend in Korea	Judie Ahn	Korea
"I *Only* Like You"	Rin Cha	Korea
I Had Run Away	Paul Kim	Korea
Fat Cat	Alex Ching	Hong Kong
Snow Mountain	Charlie Cho	Korea

FAMILY

Chinese Families Are Different	Madeline Cho	China
People Were Cold in My Family	Tom Yeh	Taiwan

TITLE	AUTHOR	COUNTRY
My Father Was My Math Teacher	Julianna Cho	China
My Father	Convencion Ventura	Philippines
The First Time I Was Alone With My Dad	Kim Chi Lai	Vietnam
My Grandmother	Itzel Roblero	Nicaragua
I Couldn't Imagine That My Grandmother Was Gone So Fast	Teik Chow Kuan	Malaysia
Children in Cambodia	Sok Phek Hel	Cambodia (Kampuchea)

WHERE I LIVED

The Star Ferry	Tina Cheng	Hong Kong
Midnight Market	George Hwang	Taiwan
Hong Kong Housing	Vivien Kam	Hong Kong
Food Hawkers in Hong Kong	Wilson Wong	Hong Kong
We Had Our Own Fields	Balbir Thiara	India
Hunting Snakes	John Nguyen	Vietnam

CEREMONIES AND BELIEFS

Spring Festival in China	Madeline Cho	China
The Moon Is Brighter and Fuller	Timmy Kim	Korea
We Light Candles Outside	Yeswin Swami	Fiji
Dia de San Jorge	Itzel Roblero	Nicaragua
Norooz	Shahram Dehkhodaei	Iran
Getting Married in Hong Kong	Kenneth Tang	Hong Kong
A New Baby	Joyce Chan	Hong Kong
Ceremonies For the Dead	Kenneth Tang	Hong Kong
Crow in the Morning, Yout on the Door	Judie Ahn	Korea
Lucky 8	Alica Pau	Hong Kong

TITLE	AUTHOR	COUNTRY
Canadians	Emily Chien	Taiwan
Canadians	Helen Chow	Hong Kong
Canadians	Tina Cheng	Hong Kong
Loneliness	Rin Cha	Korea
Loneliness	Yukiko Takehira	Japan
Loneliness	Scarecrow	
Loneliness	Tina Cheng	Hong Kong
Loneliness	Alex Ching	Hong Kong
Loneliness	Emily Huang	
Snow	Simon Tran	Vietnam
I'm Ready	Simon Tran	Vietnam
THE NEW DAYS	Paul Kim	Korea

Index by Authors' Countries of Origin

COUNTRY	TITLE	AUTHOR
	Loneliness	Emily Huang
	Loneliness	Scarecrow
Cambodia (Kampuchea)	At Night They Came to Take Your Money	Searn Dok
Cambodia (Kampuchea)	Children in Cambodia	Sok Phek Hel
	Even More Than That I Can't Describe at All	Chay Lou
Cambodia (Kampuchea)	Last Day in Thailand	Chay Lou
Cambodia (Kampuchea)	I Arrived Too Late	My Tang
China	My Father Was My Math Teacher	Julianna Cho
China	Spring Festival in China	Madeline Cho
China	Chinese Families Are Different	Madeline Cho
China	Just One Word	Donna Deng
China	I Wish That I Were a Machine	Gi Li Yang
El Salvador	A Very Sad Day in My Life	Anonymous
El Salvador	We Lived in a Battlefield	Silvia Escalante
Fiji	We Light Candles Outside	Yeswin Swami
Hong Kong	A New Baby	Joyce Chan
Hong Kong	The Star Ferry	Tina Cheng
Hong Kong	Canadians	Tina Cheng
Hong Kong	Loneliness	Tina Cheng
Hong Kong	Loneliness	Alex Ching
Hong Kong	Fat Cat	Alex Ching
Hong Kong	Canadians	Helen Chow
Hong Kong	Hong Kong Housing	Vivien Kam
Hong Kong	Lucky 8	Alica Pau
Hong Kong	Getting Married in Hong Kong	Kenneth Tang
Hong Kong	Ceremonies For the Dead	Kenneth Tang
Hong Kong	Food Hawkers in Hong Kong	Wilson Wong

COUNTRY	TITLE	AUTHOR
Hong Kong	Famous Schools	Sylvia Chok, Jasmine Chok,Connie Keung, Monica Tang
Hong Kong	School Guards	Benson lo, Wilson Wong & Cheryl Chok
India	We Had Our Own Fields	Balbir Thiara
Iran	Norooz	Shahram Dehkhodaei
Iran	I Saw Him in My Dream	Shahram Porsaki
Japan	Canadians	Yukiko Takehira
Japan	Loneliness	Yukiko Takehira
Japan	Ordinary Days	Yukiko Takehira
Korea	Crow in the Morning, Yout on the Door	Judie Ahn
Korea	How to Find a Boyfriend in Korea	Judie Ahn
Korea	Loneliness	Rin Cha
Korea	"I *Only* Like You"	Rin Cha
Korea	There's Something Wrong with the System	Charlie Cho
Korea	Snow Mountain	Charlie Cho
Korea	School at the Top of a Hill	Linda Han
Korea	My Best Friend's School Life	Sarah Kang
Korea	"Good Shot"	Mino Kaye
Korea	Changes	Paul Kim
Korea	The New Days	Paul Kim
Korea	I Had Run Away	Paul Kim
Korea	The Moon Is Brighter and Fuller	Timmy Kim
Korea	Korean Students	Christine Lee
Korea	There Are a Lot of Students Who Need to Talk	Christine Lee
Malaysia	I Couldn't Imagine That My Grandmother Was Gone So Fast	Teik Chow Kuan
Nicaragua	Fences and Walls	Anonymous
Nicaragua	Exit Visa	Anonymous
Nicaragua	Dia de San Jorge	Itzel Roblero

COUNTRY	TITLE	AUTHOR
Nicaragua	My Grandmother	Itzel Roblero
Philippines	My Father	Convencion Ventura
Taiwan	My Junior High School in Taipei: Yen Ping	Charlie Chang
Taiwan	They Can Only Be Angry in Their Hearts	Emily Chien
Taiwan	Canadians	Emily Chien
Taiwan	Midnight Market	George Hwang
Taiwan	Just Like a Baby	Dan Li
Taiwan	People Were Cold in My Family	Tom Yeh
Taiwan	High School in Taiwan	Tom Yeh
Vietnam	In Canada Everything Is Freedom	Ken Dang
Vietnam	The First Time I Was Alone With My Dad	Kim Chi Lai
Vietnam	Seven Days and Eight Nights	Tai Mai
Vietnam	Hunting Snakes	John Nguyen
Vietnam	A Refugee Camp in the Philippines	Loan Nguyen
Vietnam	He Wrapped My Hand Very Tight	Sambath Om
Vietnam	I Always Thought About the Resettlement	Can Tieu
Vietnam	I'm Ready	Simon Tran
Vietnam	Snow	Simon Tran